THE
HoW
?
BOOK SERIES

Everything in this book is factual and scientific. The most outlandish claims and stories are the most true.

Based on the design and template of Mark Wasserman and Irene Ng of Plinko, this volume was designed by Lauren LoPrete.

Manufactured in Singapore.

10 9 8 7 6 5 4 3 2 1

Library of Congress Cataloging-in-Publication Data is available.

Published by the HOW Series, Dedicated to the Exploration and Dissemination of Unbelievable Brilliance.

Photographs of Dr. and Mr. Haggis-On-Whey by Meiko Takechi Arquillos.
Cover illustration by Michael Kupperman.
Illustrations on pages 14, 15, 32, 33, 50, 51 by Ian Huebert.
Illustration on page 11 by Ryan Dodgson.
Illustration on page 53 by Miranda Currie.

This book is dedicated to: Meredith Camp, Leigh Ann Haugh, Pam Merritt, Jennifer Wegman, Julie Bagley, Diana Hamilton, Jennifer Tobin, Bonner Allen, Stephanie Hardeman, Angela Choquette, Joanna Clarke, Jan Baldwin, Angela Nash, Jennifer Knapek, Jamie Singer, Elizabeth Post, Stacey Williams, Monica Berry, Kristie Leatherberry, Katie Robbins, Angela Jones, Allison Ray, Elizabeth Porterfield, Jennifer Trulock, Hilary Shank, Allison Methvin, Kristina Whitcomb, Cindy Tonnessen, Elizabeth Gambrell, Amy Schisler, Lauren Maggard, Jenny Reynolds, Evelyn Costolo, Tiffany Lawson, Monica Pritchett, Kristen Howell, Kristin Baker, Gay Donnell, Amy Martinez, Lee Gleiser, Dana Wilcox, Paula Blackmon, Katy Spicer, Kim Brown, D'Andra Simmons, Linda Secrest, Irv Ashford, Jr., T. H. Roberto Canas, Marti Carlin, Brent Christopher, Nancy Ann Hunt, Matrice Ellis Kirk, Bill Lively, Michael Mayo, Anne Motsenbacker, Mike Rawlings, David M. Rosenberg, Julia Simon, Paula Strasser, Don Williams Meredith Camp, Leigh Ann Haugh, Pam Merritt, Jennifer Wegman, Julie Bagley, Diana Hamilton, Jennifer Tobin, Bonner Allen, Stephanie Hardeman, Angela Choquette, Joanna Clarke, Jan Baldwin, Angela Nash, Jennifer Knapek, Jamie Singer, Elizabeth Post, Stacey Williams, Monica Berry, Kristie Leatherberry, Katie Robbins, Angela Jones, Allison Ray, Elizabeth Porterfield, Jennifer Trulock, Hilary Shank, Allison Methvin, Kristina Whitcomb, Cindy Tonnessen, Elizabeth Gambrell, Amy Schisler, Lauren Maggard, Jenny Reynolds, Evelyn Costolo, Tiffany Lawson, Monica Pritchett, Kristen Howell, Kristin Baker, Gay Donnell, Amy Martinez, Lee Gleiser, Dana Wilcox, Paula Blackmon, Katy Spicer, Kim Brown, D'Andra Simmons, Linda Secrest, Irv Ashford, Jr., T. H. Roberto Canas, Marti Carlin, Brent Christopher, Nancy Ann Hunt, Matrice Ellis Kirk, Bill Lively, Michael Mayo, Anne Motsenbacker, Mike Rawlings, David M. Rosenberg, Julia Simon, Paula Strasser, Don Williams

Please visit:
www.foreignpolicy.com
www.mcsweeneys.net

ISBN 978-1-934781-21-0

The
HAGGIS-ON-WHEY
WORLD
of
UNBELIEVABLE
BRILLIANCE
PRESENTS
CHILDREN
and the
TUNDRA
[VOLUME 112]
MMIVIIIIII

DR. AND MR. DORIS HAGGIS-ON-WHEY'S WORLD OF UNBELIEVABLE BRILLIANCE

Dear Reader,

Well, this is a new low. Our longtime publisher, apparently named after some bar in Boston, has forced us into an ignominious and unconscionable corner. For years we have delivered to them texts of incomparable brilliance, and presumably we've brought them immeasurable wealth and prestige. And though they seem barely able to zip their Members Only jackets without cutting themselves, all this time they seemed, at least, to have been able to somehow print and distribute books.

But that era has passed. Now they tell us that due to "budget cuts" and "unforeseen issues of national security," we must combine two books into one. It is as ludicrous a notion as has ever been proposed, more ludicrous than Cincinnati or deodorant. Shame showers us all.

As you know, the books in the Haggis-on-Whey series now number in the mid-hundreds, and the order of these books has been carefully planned. The stunning success of our last book, *Cold Fusion*, was to be followed, logically, by a book about the terrible subject of Children. And that was to be followed by a welcome palate cleanser, an exploration of that most beguiling of biomes, the Tundra.

But due to the economic incompetencies of this fly-by-night publishing outfit, to cut costs, we have been forced to combine both books into this single volume. What's worse, a number of pages have been sold to some group in Australia selling not Australian goods or services, but selling Australians themselves.

All of this makes a mockery of our work.

We curse the seeds of capitalism. We curse the winds of commerce.

And we blame you for your complicity.

Dr. and Mr. Doris Haggis-On-Whey

CHILDREN: KEY PARTS TO KNOW AND AVOID

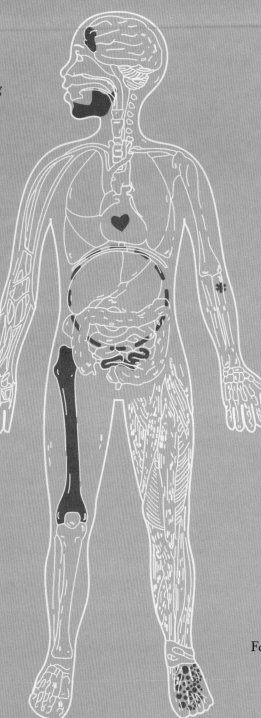

PREFRONTAL CORTEX
For plotting schemes; for developing whines; for making excuses; for avoiding all accountability.

HEART
For twisting; for withholding; for hiding; for facilitating solar eclipses.

RIGHT ARM
For tugging; for imploring, grasping, attention-getting; for incongruous gesturing while screaming.

STOMACH
Like a regular stomach, except equipped with tools to induce grass fires and maximize whining.

BURROWING BONE
For burrowing.

JAWS
Able to engulf and swallow all meaning and reason.

LEFT ARM
For the storage of excess bile.

LIVER AND KIDNEY
For the processing of fake tears, fake apologies, fake regrets, fake gratitude, fake appreciation for their elders; for science; for the science pioneered by their grandmother, whom everyone else seems to appreciate just fine.

MITOUNAMPHIBIAS
For harboring demon larvae.

MANIPULATION

GUILT

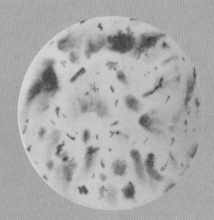

SHIRKING OF RESPONSIBILITY

THE EIGHT MAIN KINDS OF TUNDRA

Sunny Tundra

Midnight Tundra

1943 Tundra

Nearsighted Tundra

Golden-Hour Tundra

Tundra After Spinning Around

Another Picture of Tundra

Tundra on Television

EARLY SIGHTINGS OF CHILDREN AND WHAT PEOPLE THOUGHT WHEN THEY SAW THEM

Children seem to be everywhere in our modern times, but there was a time, not long ago, when we lived in a world without children. In fact, the earliest record of children seems to be 1645, in the diary of Francisco de Naranja, a monk living in Costa de los Perros, France. "Today I saw a curious creature," wrote the French monk, in English. "It was similar to a monkey, but hairless and less intelligent. It was small, ugly, covered in dirt and with pointed ears. For hours I tried to capture it with a butterfly net, but it eluded me. I think I shall call this creature Devil Monkey."

A few months later, villagers 100 miles west saw a similar small group of these Devil Monkeys crawling from a low-slung cave in the side of a hill. The creatures were naked and asking for snacks.

From then on, the sightings of Devil Monkeys — or children, as they are now known — increased steadily. Even as townspeople tried to drive them away with brooms and spoiled meats, the Devil Monkeys grew stronger and bolder. They ventured onto farms to steal vegetables and wheat. They begged for soap or shelter. They pulled off daring affection heists.

But as with the cicada, you can only successfully fight off so many children in the course of a day. Eventually their numbers and stench will wear you down.

And so, with furrowed brows and clenched fists, the citizens welcomed children into their lives. Or, at least, into their sheds. Or, put more accurately, the villagers welcomed the children into the smaller, cheaper sheds they built behind the adult sheds. These child-sheds helped mitigate some of the stench, and did a fair job of muffling the screeching.

IMPORTANT LAYERS OF THE TUNDRA

LAYER ONE: "THE YELLOW SNOW LAYER"

Home to the small ecosystem that lives in and subsists on musk-ox urine.

LAYER TWO: "THE SEMI-PERMAFROST"

So labeled because of its waffly nature. A popular destination for caribou looking to hide their young.

LAYER THREE: "THE PERMAFROST"

A seedy layer corrupted by greedy ice profiteers and teenage moles. Not a destination for visitors.

LAYER FOUR: "THE SUB-PERMAFROST"

Even worse than, and below, the permafrost.

LAYER FIVE: "FROZEN ENTREE BACKSTOCK LAYER"

Despite their public acceptance of a non-proliferation treaty, Hungry Man still keeps large, secret deposits of microwaveable meals down here.

LAYER SIX: "THE ICE CUBE MINES"

The work site of thousands of tiny baby ermine offspring exploited for their quiet demeanor and fast, skilled claws. With world ice-cube consumption on the rise, this corrupt practice will most likely continue unabated.

LAYER SEVEN: "THE FROZEN FIRST CLASS"

Where the Arctic's highest-profile movers and shakers go to let their hair down.

LAYER EIGHT: "THE MEANING OF IT ALL LAYER"

There's only one place where it feels this mellow. Where it feels this right. Where you can wear a ribbed turtleneck and everyone knows exactly what you mean. Come on down, and don't book a return trip. Steve is not here so it will be okay.

A GUIDE TO CLIPPING YOUR CHILD'S WINGS

First off — as you will soon find out if you try a do-it-yourself approach — garden shears WILL NOT get the job done. No man-made scissors are up to the task.

Unlike the soft, feathery wings of a bird, a child's wings are made out of a dense, flexible cartilage that is virtually impervious to saws and blades. Also, if you wait until your child's wings have matured too much, it may be nearly impossible to remove them. Then you'll be forced to send them to Eriterisha, the Mediterranean bird-child state. And no parent wants that, because they bill you monthly and the charges for phone use and cleanings are exorbitant.

CAUTION: If your attic has become a nest for your child and his or her bird offspring, it's TOO LATE. You have passed the wing-removal stage. Good luck dealing with your permanent child-bird.

Step 1: Sedate your child. You can find the appropriate high-strength animal tranquilizers in the supply closets of most zoos, or through online retailers in Canada.

Step 2: Summon the wings. This can be accomplished by whispering, "Rise, great spawns of misevolution! RISE!" Or by gently lifting them.

Step 3: Cut along the dotted line. Look carefully at the place where your child's wings meet their backs, and you'll find a clear dotted line. Dip one of those tiny brushes that come with most bottles of nail polish into a hot fondue pot filled with old Greek yogurt. Paint a stripe of old hot yogurt along the dotted line. Allow the yogurt to dry, and the wings will snap off easily.

Step 4: Cover your tracks. Take the time to properly dispose of your child's wings. Trusting someone like Randy Foye to dispose of the wings is a surefire way to arouse suspicion from your newly un-birded offspring. Don't cut corners with your child's wings. Hire someone besides Randy Foye.

Step 5: Tell the child you love it. They expect you to say this, and they seem to enjoy it. It will help you lull them into a stupor, during which time you will make your escape.

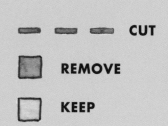

- - - **CUT**

■ **REMOVE**

□ **KEEP**

SOME INTERESTING REAL ESTATE OPPORTUNITIES IN THE TUNDRA

COZY CHARMER This rustic snuggler is close to snow, cold, wind, *and* ice. Fire-burning stove, wood floors, some new shingles. Dirt floors stay cool year-round.

EVER WANT TO GET AWAY? Approx 30 sq ft of midcentury comfort on Siberia's exclusive Lena Delta. Perfect for loners, hermits, Catholics. All fixtures original. Says FISH in big letters along east side.

"THE WORKS" For those who want something unique. Comes with satellite dish, three plastic chairs, Canadian flag, and one-of-a-kind front step apparatus that can be raised and lowered for no discernible reason.

ULTRAMODERN DESIGN Noted Danish architect Hans Blook's masterwork, nicknamed "Brown Box." Outside, clean lines and beautiful silhouette. Inside, 38 sq ft, everything painted brown. Outside also brown.

VIEWS FOR MILES Unobstructed views of grass, sky, rocks, moss. Innovative "slanted" roof design allows rain and snow to fall off, onto the ground, instead of remaining on the roof.

BRAND-NEW CONSTRUCTION Last available shack on the Kerguelen Islands' hot Rallier du Baty peninsula. This one has it all — four walls, two windows, four red doors. Marsh location ensures access to water.

You Can't Have a Party without... an Australian™

It's Better with an Australian™

People have tried to party without one, but the results have been bleak.

Do not take tea with Australians if you take nitrates, often prescribed for chest pain, as this may cause a sudden, unsafe drop in blood pressure. Discuss your general health status with your doctor to ensure that you are healthy enough to engage with an Australian. If you experience chest pain, nausea, or any other discomforts during your time with an Australian, seek immediate medical help. In the rare instance of a social engagement with an Australian lasting more than four hours, seek immediate medical attention to avoid long-term injury. If you are older than 65, or have serious liver or kidney problems, your doctor may start you with fewer Australians. If you are taking protease inhibitors, your doctor may limit you to a maximum of one Australian in a 24-hour period. In rare instances, Australians will cause a sudden decrease in or loss of vision. The most common side effects of Australians are headache, facial flushing, bluish vision, and sensitivity to light. You are encouraged to report negative side effects of Australians to the Australian Department of Labor, and to Andrew Adamson.

THE STRANGE AND OFTEN CONTRADICTORY FOOD CHAIN OF THE TUNDRA

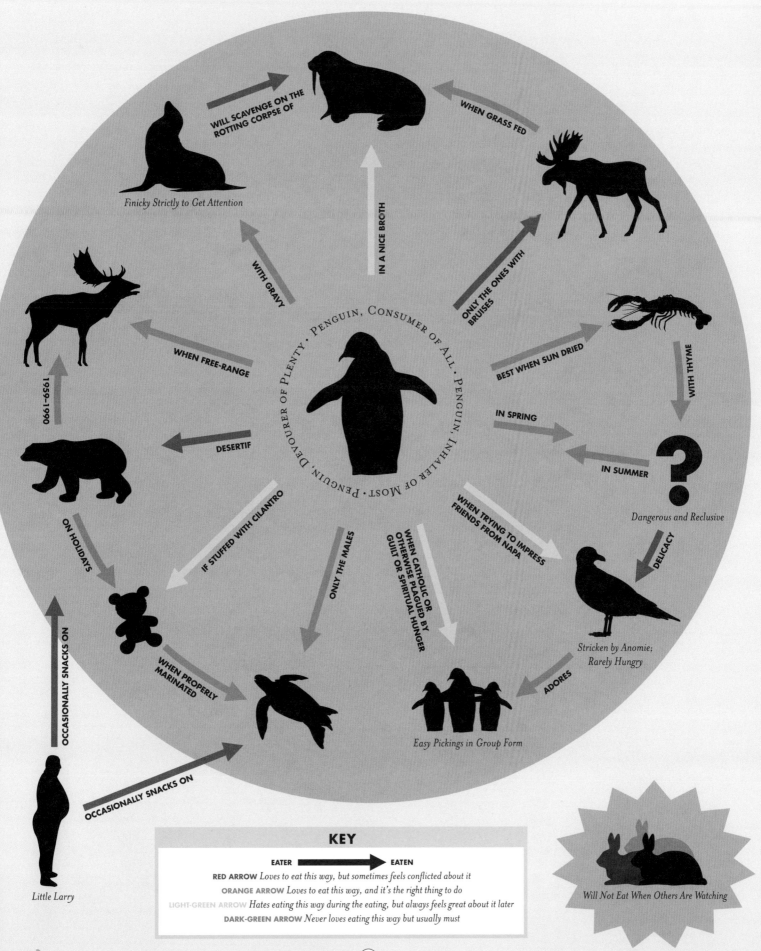

PENGUIN, CONSUMER OF ALL · PENGUIN, INHALER OF MOST · PENGUIN, DEVOURER OF MOST · PENGUIN, DEVOURER OF PLENTY ·

WILL SCAVENGE ON THE ROTTING CORPSE OF

WHEN GRASS FED

Finicky Strictly to Get Attention

IN A NICE BROTH

WITH GRAVY

ONLY THE ONES WITH BRUISES

WHEN FREE-RANGE

BEST WHEN SUN DRIED

WITH THYME

1959–1990

DESERTIF

IN SPRING

IN SUMMER

Dangerous and Reclusive

OCCASIONALLY SNACKS ON

ON HOLIDAYS

IF STUFFED WITH CILANTRO

ONLY THE MALES

WHEN CATHOLIC OR OTHERWISE PLAGUED BY GUILT OR SPIRITUAL HUNGER

WHEN TRYING TO IMPRESS FRIENDS FROM NAPA

DELICACY

WHEN PROPERLY MARINATED

ADORES

Stricken by Anomie; Rarely Hungry

OCCASIONALLY SNACKS ON

Easy Pickings in Group Form

Little Larry

Will Not Eat When Others Are Watching

KEY

EATER ➔ EATEN

RED ARROW *Loves to eat this way, but sometimes feels conflicted about it*
ORANGE ARROW *Loves to eat this way, and it's the right thing to do*
LIGHT-GREEN ARROW *Hates eating this way during the eating, but always feels great about it later*
DARK-GREEN ARROW *Never loves eating this way but usually must*

SNOW DRUIDS: FACT AND FICTION

Always I have to hear about snow druids. When I mentioned to some of the villagers who live near me and smell like wheat that I was writing about the tundra, all of them wanted to know about the druids. Tell me about the snow druids! Are they real? On and on, babbling and drooling while smelling like wheat. For them and for you, here are answers to the common perceptions and misperceptions and other ludicrous things you might think.

They pretend they don't watch TV.
FACT. This is an instinctive, inherited trait of snow druids that they all take on from birth. It also has no evolutionary basis at all.

None have siblings.
FACT. A female snow druid can only breed once in her life, making the prospect of a "dud" child that much more worrisome. However, for the price of a few pounds of bear meat, a snow druid shaman will pretend to see through the mother's pregnant belly to check on the growth of the offspring, much like a farmer checking on a young calf. Unfortunately, unlike farmers, snow druid parents get no government subsidies for failed crops. Just a gangly kid wearing a hood.

Snow druids make their own capes.
FICTION. Snow druids wear capes tailored by a community of otherwise unemployed tailors in Breckenridge, Colorado.

They at least DESIGN their own capes, though, right? Or suggest the fabric?
FICTION. The snow druid cape-making process is entirely out of their hands. Leave it alone.

They are not fun to play goofs on.
FACT *and* FICTION. Unlike many of the other inhabitants of the tundra — many of whom have even developed entirely goof-based economies — the druids abhor goofs. Occasionally, an extremely happy-go-lucky snow druid can be joshed with (by permission). But straight-up goofing is never advised. However, as druids grow older, their goof aversion worsens significantly, especially in their autumn years. At this point, a skilled goofer can, with proper coordination and planning,

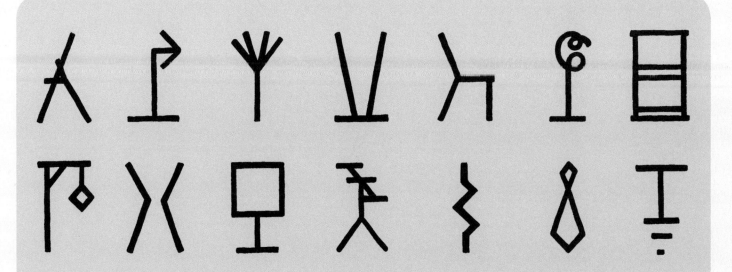

ABOVE: Ancient snow druid etchings discovered outside France's French-Canadian embassy. This short phrase or poem has been translated many times by different professors and snow druid historians. Over time, scholars have agreed it can be interpreted one of two ways, depending on how you rate the angle on the sixth symbol's swirl. Either the phrase reads, "Never let our people be washed from this earth," or "Don't tell Uncle about the floor." Either way it's an excellent example of an advanced dingbat-based language and the amazingly straight lines that one can make with only four shortened wooden nubs for hands.

try a burned-toast-in-the-shoe goof, a Pop-Rocks-in-the-light-bulbs goof, and possibly even a your-dental-surgeon-is-actually-your-grocer goof. All others are still, at present time, thought to be imprudent.

Snow druids only read books featuring dog protagonists.
FACT. They have read all the major dog-protagonist book series, especially those involving very small dogs who nonetheless accomplish great things through their sense of smell and their ability to bargain with merchants, both honest and Southern.

Snow druids are neither nocturnal nor day...turnal.
FACT. And the opposite of nocturnal is diurnal. Snow druids operate on a highly sophisticated sleep schedule that depends on the season; the town they live in; the foods they've eaten that day; the wind; their gender; their pants size; their shoe size; the length of their surname; and whether or not their fickle god of sleep, Sergio Ghilotti, has commanded them to slumber or not.

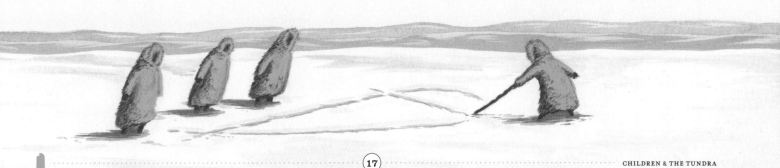

QUICK FIXES FOR THE GROWING EPIDEMIC OF TALKING CHILD SYNDROME

You did everything right. You gave it shelter; you fed and watered your child. You performed every task you were supposed to. But then one day something went wrong. It started speaking. What can you do? The first thing to realize is that *you are not alone*. The second thing to realize is that the color of the paper on this page is mauve. It is pronounced with a long *o*.

In the last 20 years, some combination of free radicals in our food and wicker in our homes has caused a sharp increase in Talking Child Syndrome. There are, however, ways to bring your child back to its natural, silent, state. The following are questions and answers you should read if you are reading this book and would like to continue reading the words on this page, which is mauve.

STEP 1: **Have you been soaking it long enough?**
Perhaps you think you are too busy to soak your child for the recommended 80 minutes daily. Perhaps you are thinking of cutting corners by simply rinsing your child off with a bucket or watering can. Do not. A good long soaking subdues children's powers of speech, keeping them drowsy and confused about what to say or why they exist.

STEP 2: **Have you tried sleeping it in the hallway or laundry room?** These places will discourage the formation of words and other mouth sounds.

STEP 3: **Has it been exposed to too many things to talk about?** Keeping it in a simple room without objects or colors will limit the things it will want to notice or comment on.

STEP 4: **Are there any leaks in its nighttime child case?** There can be no leaks in its nighttime child case.

HOW CHILDREN USE THEIR HORRIBLE VOICES TO DESTROY THE NATURAL WORLD

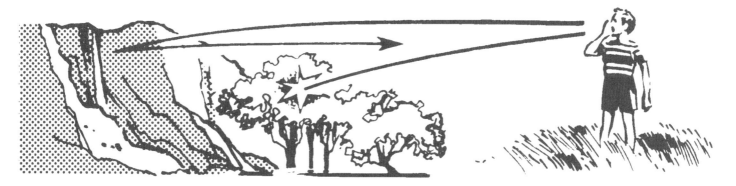

Children are equipped with a number of weapons to ensure the propagation of their species. Their looks are horrible and will induce vomiting in other animals. Their clothing is disgusting. Their fingernails are always brown and stink of their own armpits. But there is one feature of children more deadly — and potentially world-ending — than any other: their terrible, shrill voices, which debase the earth and threaten to tear tectonic plates asunder. Scientists, except myself, have no idea why children would want to destroy the world by talking and sometimes talking loudly. When they do, mountains tumble and the seas boil with filth and vermin. And why do children do this? Why do they open their unspeakable mouths? They seem to do it willfully. Our Armed Forces try gallantly to stop children from making their wretched noises, but right now there are too many children, and most of these children have mouths. Thus for the time being we will endure the sounds they emit, and our trees, hills, and glaciers will fall.

SIMPLIFIED RESEARCH ILLUSTRATES WHY THE ALPINE TUNDRA SHOULD BE ERADICATED FROM THE PANTHEON OF GREAT TUNDRAS.

SCORING THE TUNDRAS

	Arctic	Alpine	Antarctic
Subsoil Is Permafrost	✓		✓
Land Is Flat	✓		✓
Air Is Cold	✓	✓	✓
Wind Is Windy	✓	✓	✓
Caribou	✓		
Malaise	✓		
Musk Ox	✓		
Seals			✓
Polar Bears	✓		
Rabbits			✓
Penguins			✓
Lemmings	✓		
Dwarf Shrubs		✓	
Inferiority Complex		✓	
Lichen	✓	✓	✓
Reindeer	✓		
Fancy Ice (unsculpted)			✓
Fancy Ice (sculpted)	✓		✓
Lagoons	✓		✓
Santa	✓		
Severity	✓	✓	✓
Sadness		✓	
Tax Shelters			✓
Hypothermia	✓	✓	✓
Sports Radio			✓
John Lithgow in Drag		✓	

BENNY'S ZONE

These pages are court-ordered and make Benny so happy.

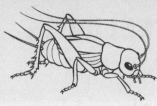
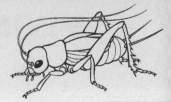

MY UNDERSTANDING OF THE GAME OF CRICKET

Someone decides who's the main guy. He gets the rubber thing. Everyone else goes to their spot. The people watching watch. Sometimes if you're wearing white you start running. Nobody takes a bathroom break. Except me and when I do there's water in bowls EVERYWHERE.

If you're wearing a mask and you're done wearing it you should give it to the next guy. He'll usually put it on. Music comes on. It's never the alphabet song. When you hit one hand with the other it's clapping but it might hurt. No one ever wants you to do it though. Except you. But you stop.

Sometimes the rubber thing goes high, high, high, high into the air. And really near you. And then disappears right above your head.

When you wake up, your eye is blueberry colored. And you're wearing a steak eye patch. This is the best kind of eye patch. DON'T EAT IT. Instead eat a different steak. You can tell it's cooked if someone gives it to you.

And stay up late. You're the captain of the ice cream brigade! Sound your big horn so everyone knows you're coming. You just did some cricket.

BENNY'S TIMELINE OF ALL HUMANKIND

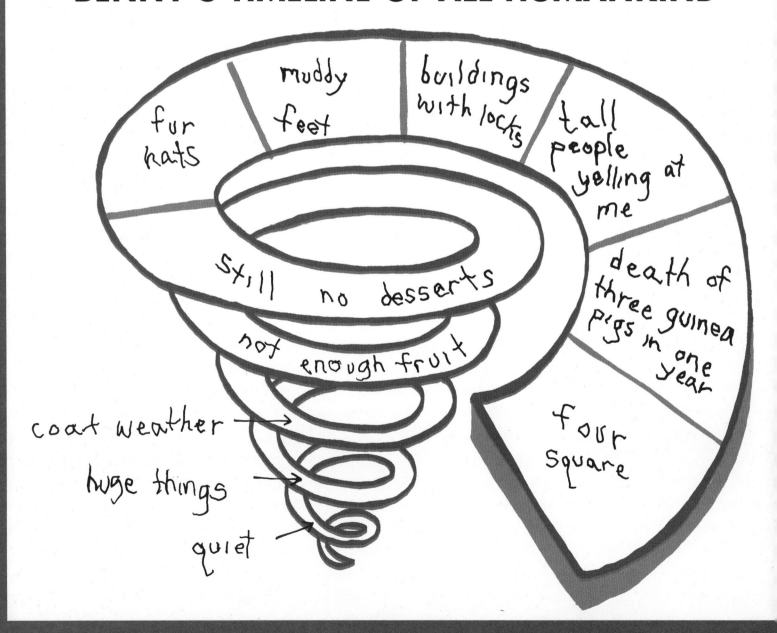

MIXING TIME!

First off, be a boy. Second, wear a blue shirt. Third, open your eyes. Now use them to look at some white thing in your hand. Have fun. If you're now having fun then you're doing it right. Keep going.

Grab the spoon on the table. Actually, maybe put that down. Who put a spoon there? It might be there for a reason. Is there a way to find out? Probably not. No one ever explains spoons to me.

Hold up the white thing in your hand again. Has it changed yet? It probably has. Whew. You're done. You did it!

I love you too and am tired.

BENNY'S FEELINGS FOR BUNNIES

Different bunnies make Benny feel different ways. Match up the photo of Benny with the bunny he's seen.

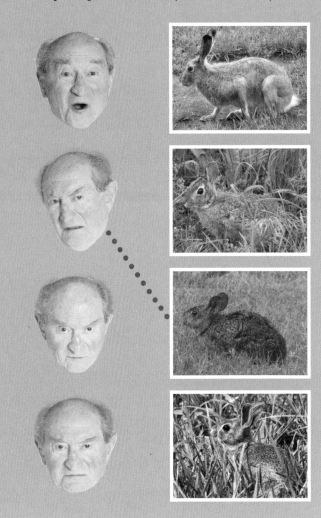

HOW TO MAKE THE MOST OF YOUR TIMEOUT

Oh, no, you're in that corner again. Staring straight at the wall. You can do these things if you want:

1. *Compare yourself to yourself.* A second ago you weren't in a timeout. Now you are. Are you the same person you were then, or are you two different people, and do the different people like the same things, like bread?

2. *You're stuck in a chair but most of the time you can still move your feet.* So that means you can kick them together. Oh, no, they're fighting! See who's going to win. If you know, don't tell anyone. It's mean to spoil things for people who don't know.

3. *You can wonder about pinecones.* They're hard to figure out. Where are they from? They're hard like wood. Not good at talking. Good at holding on to branches. Do you think we'll always have them? Where are they from?

4. *Take a break.*

5. *Dr. Doris doesn't allow flowers in the house.* She says they're just colored weeds. I don't think I know how to do this number. I have eaten three things today that Doris didn't want me to eat. One of them was regular food.

HOW TO TELL THE MOUNTAINS FROM THE SKY

Go up to both of them. Mountains can be touched but then when you're standing on them they disappear. Skies can't ever be touched, no matter how close you get. And sometimes they disappear when you're in bed or when the window is closed. The differences between mountains and sky can be hard to remember but most of it is about touching.

"IT'S COMPLICATED": MY RELATIONSHIP WITH DOGS

FIVE BEST PLACES TO HIDE A PLASTIC BAG

In other bags

Near snow

It's okay if they're not hidden

Under people

In mountains

CONNECT FOUR

Find a friend. Decide who's red and who's black. Take turns. Every time two reds or two blacks are in a line then that's good. Don't talk! No talking! Crush all words like ants! CRUSH THEM CRUSH THEM LIKE BUGS?

BENNY HAS A DOLLAR!

Benny has found a dollar! What should he do with it? Close your eyes and put your finger down. What did you point to? Wherever your finger hand landed is what Benny should spend a dollar on. Now give Benny a dollar.

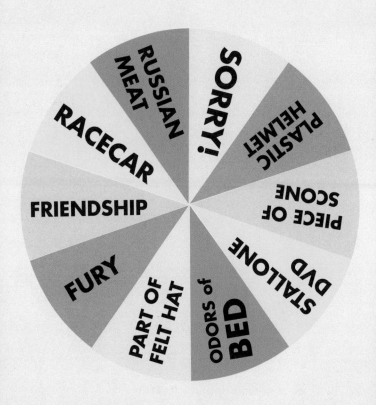

RUSSIAN MEAT · SORRY! · PLASTIC HELMET · RACECAR · PIECE OF SCONE · FRIENDSHIP · STALLONE DVD · FURY · ODORS of BED · PART OF FELT HAT

BENNY'S REVIEWS

BRAND A
These ones are okay.
I got to use these one time.
I used them for wiping.

MOISTNESS: Four.
FINAL PART: I'm going to use these again, probably. They're white like other baby wipes (AT FIRST). Terrible as blankets. Too wet. And small. Smelled like the bubble water Dr. Doris keeps on the counter.

BRAND B
These ones are good.
I've used them.
They're baby wipes.

MOISTNESS: Four.
WIPEYNESS: Three.
BOX-COLOR FUNNESS: One.
FINAL PART: I would wipe with this baby wipe again if someone let me.

BRAND C
Not sure about these ones.
Never seen or used them before.

WIPEYNESS: Four.
BOX-COLOR FUNNESS: Four.
FINAL PART: I really like liking these. I could right now even. Good for pets. And good to use on pets. Give them a girl's name, like Chrissy. Please let's name it Chrissy.

Every Smart Business Needs... an Australian™

It's Better with an Australian™

Important Facts About Australians to be considered:

Great with team sports (company or otherwise); willing smilers; fearless in battle; can only be killed by special swords forged in Ancient times; no issues with slaying enemies while they sleep; good penmanship; excellent note-takers; if they so choose, they can be undetectable to the naked eye; good with the elderly; adept with most spreadsheet programs; disobedient but loyal; sometimes immortal; most can swim.

Do not take Australians if you take nitrates, often prescribed for chest pain, as this may cause a sudden, unsafe drop in blood pressure. Discuss your general health status with your doctor to ensure that you are healthy enough to engage with an Australian. If you experience chest pain, nausea, or any other discomforts during your time with an Australian, seek immediate medical help. In the rare instance of an Australian lasting more than four hours, seek immediate medical help to avoid long-term injury. If you are older than 65, or have serious liver or kidney problems, your doctor may start you at the lowest dose of Australians. If you are taking protease inhibitors, your doctor may limit you to a maximum single dose of Australian in a 24-hour period. In rare instances, Australians will cause a sudden decrease in or loss of vision. It is not possible to determine whether these events are related directly to Australians or to other factors. Australians should not be used in conjunction with other Pacific Rim peoples. The most common side effects of Australians are headache, facial flushing, bluish vision, and sensitivity to light. You are encouraged to report negative side effects of Australians to the Australian Department of Labor, and to Andrew Adamson.

DEALING WITH CHILD AUDITORS

So… some of those tax loopholes weren't quite as large as they looked at first glance. Now you're stuck inside one of them, barely able to wiggle your fingers, and a 51-inch auditor in a cheap linen suit is staring you down. What do you do?

SOME GUIDELINES:

No compliments. Sweet talk makes child tax auditors angry.

Do not try to deduct stationery. Using paper to write off paper expenses is an irony not lost on them.

Provide dip. A good dip, served in a colorful bowl, sends a message that you are serious, yes, but that you care about dip and putting it into colorful bowls. It's okay if Steve gives you the bowl.

Use proper paper presentation. The Eastern style is no longer appropriate, and very well might provoke their wrath. The Cambridge style of tax document delivery is now most common. First, lower yourself to one knee, drop your head, and adopt the "swan's itch" position, hiding your face in your armpit. Now, keeping your back parallel to the ground, present your paperwork with your right hand. Once accepted by your auditor, let go and release yourself into the "fallen snowflake" position, humming.

Always offer a gift. Doesn't need to be expensive, but should be something mantel worthy. Actually, just get something expensive.

PIE CHARTS SUBMITTED BY CHILDREN

THE SMELL OF CHILDREN IN ART HISTORY

The odor emitted by children has been documented by scientists, mused about by poets, and discussed fruitlessly by philosophers. But no one has better explored how and why children smell as they do better than the world's great painters, all of them dead. Let us explore some of these:

DIEGO VELÁZQUEZ *LAS MENINAS* 1656 Velázquez painted more than two dozen canvases dedicated to the smell of children, none of them very good. This was one of the better ones. It was frowned upon by the academy and Velázquez was forced into exile, which is where he belonged because he was a sucky painter.

NICOLAS POUSSIN *THE HOLY FAMILY ON THE STEPS* 1648 Poussin, who talked like a macaw, said he wanted to get to the core of the phenomenon of child odor. Instead he painted this abomination. He died far too late.

JOSEPH BLACKBURN *THE WINSLOW FAMILY* 1755 An example of early American art, all of which was bad. None of these paintings should have been painted. Americans made everyone look oblong and pale, and their torsos far too long. And those stubby hands!

MARY CASSATT *THE BATH* 1891 Considered one of our best artists, she was still pretty bad. I could have done better, and I'm a scientist. I don't understand why this picture was created, or why we're looking at it.

MARC CHAGALL *THE BABY'S BATH* 1916 This one is kind of a joke, right? Nothing looks right. Are they in a boat on high seas? Why is everything crooked? Is that supposed to be a puddle at the bottom? This one makes me laugh and then makes me very, very angry.

When You Need a Colonoscopy, You Need...
an Australian™

It's Better with an Australian™

This delicate procedure is never enjoyable, and can often hurt a good deal. But things are bound to go better if it's performed, or at least witnessed by, an AUSTRALIAN.

Do not take Australians if you take nitrates, often prescribed for chest pain, as this may cause a sudden, unsafe drop in blood pressure. Discuss your general health status with your doctor to ensure that you are healthy enough to engage with an Australian. If you experience chest pain, nausea, or any other discomforts during your time with an Australian, seek immediate medical help. In the rare instance of an Australian lasting more than four hours, seek immediate medical help to avoid long-term injury. If you are older than 65, or have serious liver or kidney problems, your doctor may start you at the lowest dose of Australians. If you are taking protease inhibitors, your doctor may limit you to a maximum single dose of Australian in a 24-hour period. In rare instances, Australians will cause a sudden decrease in or loss of vision. It is not possible to determine whether these events are related directly to Australians or to other factors. Australians should not be used in conjunction with other Pacific Rim peoples. The most common side effects of Australians are headache, facial flushing, bluish vision, and sensitivity to light. You are encouraged to report negative side effects of Australians to the Australian Department of Labor, and to Andrew Adamson.

COMPARING SNOW WITH PRESIDENTS PAST AND PRESENT

SNOW	ZACHARY TAYLOR	SNOW	CHESTER ARTHUR
• COLD • WHITE • USUALLY ON THE GROUND	• COLD • WHITE • USUALLY ON THE GROUND	• COLD • WHITE • FLEETING	• COLD • WHITE • FLEETING

SNOW	HERBERT HOOVER	SNOW	GERALD FORD
• COLD • WHITE • TEMPORARY	• COLD • WHITE • ALLITERATIVE	• COLD • WHITE • FALLING GENTLY	• COLD • WHITE • FALLING OFTEN

HERE ARE SOME PICTURES OF CHILDREN WHO ARE HAPPY TO HAVE BEEN PUNISHED FOR THEIR MISDEEDS, AND WHO HAVE LEARNED MUCH FROM THEIR JUSTLY METED-OUT PUNISHMENT:

"I'm sorry."

"So sorry."

"I feel so bad."

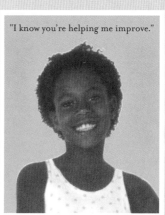

"I know you're helping me improve."

HOW CHILDREN MIGHT POISON YOU

They have the technology. But why would they do this — why would they want to poison you? What I have been able to discover is that, above all, it's nothing personal. Children don't really care enough about you to invest the energy in poisoning you out of some sense of revenge or whatnot. This is a crucial thing to understand about children, that their constant squeals of "joy" and "happiness" mask their deep and unending ennui. And so they experiment with explosives, code breaking, and, most of all, poisons. Your best strategy for living among them while remaining unpoisoned is to be vigilant about everything you eat, touch, and breathe. They specialize in inhalants, and these of course cannot be seen. Thus you could be breathing in poison at any moment, whether or not a child is nearby. They also know how to get into the municipal water supply. Also they don't sleep and they work very hard.

CLIP 'N' SAVE

WARNING SIGNS YOU MIGHT BE POISONED BY A CHILD:

- You cannot breathe.

- Your organs are failing.

- You are floating above your corpse.

- You are some kind of ghost, attending your own funeral, watching your friends and relatives give you halfhearted eulogies.

- You are floating heavenward, your soul shedding its human form, becoming one with air and space, a ray of pure light.

- You hear the mirthless laughter of a child, happy to have brought about your demise.

Some common poisons favored by children.

IMPORTANT ANNOUNCEMENT: CHILDREN POSING AS PEOPLE

Of course they try to infiltrate. They need supplies. They lust for power. They prefer our clothes and deodorants to their natural furs and oils. So we must be vigilant. We must avoid public pools. And documentaries. Look for these signs:

DO THEY TALK TO WOMEN HOLDING RED PURSES WHILE IT'S RAINING IN FRONT OF RED-ROOFED RANCH HOUSES, AS IF THE WHOLE THING, THE WHOLE TRAGIC MESS OF IT ALL, DOESN'T GIVE THEM AWAY IN A SECOND? WHAT A JOKE.

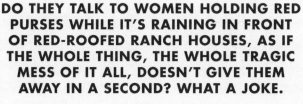

DO THEY WEAR SAFARI KHAKIS AND HOLD SHOVELS AND ACT ALL BOSSY WHEN YOU'RE JUST TRYING TO WEAR YOUR NEW UGGS AND HOLD YOUR MAP?

DO THEY CONTROL YOUR LIFE WHILE PRETENDING YOU CONTROL THEIRS?

IN THE SHADOW OF THE ELVEN SWEATSHOP: A LOOK AT SANTA'S NEIGHBORS

THERE ARE MANY CURIOSITIES TO ADDRESS WHEN THINKING OF SAINT NICK. WHERE DOES HE HOUSE ALL HIS WORKERS? WHERE'S HE GETTING ALL THAT PLASTIC AND RUBBER? ARE ELVEN HOLIDAYS OBSERVED, AND IF SO, TO WHAT DEGREE? WHY CAN'T ANYONE GET A LOOK AT HIS ACCOUNTING BOOKS? WHY RED?

ONE QUESTION BEGGED FURTHER INQUIRY ABOVE ALL OTHERS: WHO ARE SANTA'S NEIGHBORS? WHOSE QUIET LIVES WERE UPENDED BY SANTA'S BULLDOZING ARRIVAL?

1. KILGARD FRANK Born of rich, Viking blood, Kilgard has a soft, delicate nature and is a lover of all forms of miniature transportation toys. Besides a robust train set, Kilgard owns one of the world's finest English miniature metro sets, which runs on the exact same schedule as England's. Sure, he's had a misfire here or there what with the regrettable mini-Segway village or the tedious hand-bike off-road course, but the world of tiny transportation toys has never been one for those prone to destructive hindsighting. He also makes a mint selling still-life paintings of pasta.

2. AGNUS MURMA Spice maker and glüg enthusiast. Has an extensive knowledge of all kinds of Egyptian cotton and has also been found not guilty in six cases of reindeer drugging. Her pleasant, sweet disposition happens to be buried under layers and layers of impenetrable, encrusted, cantankerous bile. Usual Sundays consist of listening to a nice recording of a dial tone or single-note humming compilations. Her best nights end with the burning of something valuable.

3. PAT TOLEMAN A quiet homebody fond of both dusting and sweeping. Has a modest 1 1/2 bedroom and a promising leek garden. Interesting fact about Pat: the only part of him that ages is his feet. These resemble those of a 195-year-old man. This fact renders walking impossible, as well as most day-to-day functions. But watch him play Boggle; he's a verifiable word shark. He is also a quiet homebody fond of both sweeping and also dusting. Thus his surname.

4. THE LARSENS Recent transplants from Boca Raton. They might be moving soon.

5. ED AND TEX Prolific salmon fishermen, moved to the North to try their hands at ice holing. Renowned for their "no bait" fishing technique, as well as for their lack of success. Quick to anger, especially after fishing (which is common Tuesday–Monday). Combine this with their pungent caribou cologne, and they find themselves routinely avoided by the townspeople. Except on shampoo Thursdays.

6. LARRY The town cheat. Smells like cheap condiments. Stingy with stationery. Loves nothing better than a good grapple. Except for television murder, which is better, as long as they get the blood right.

5 MOST COMMON KID THOUGHTS BY AGE

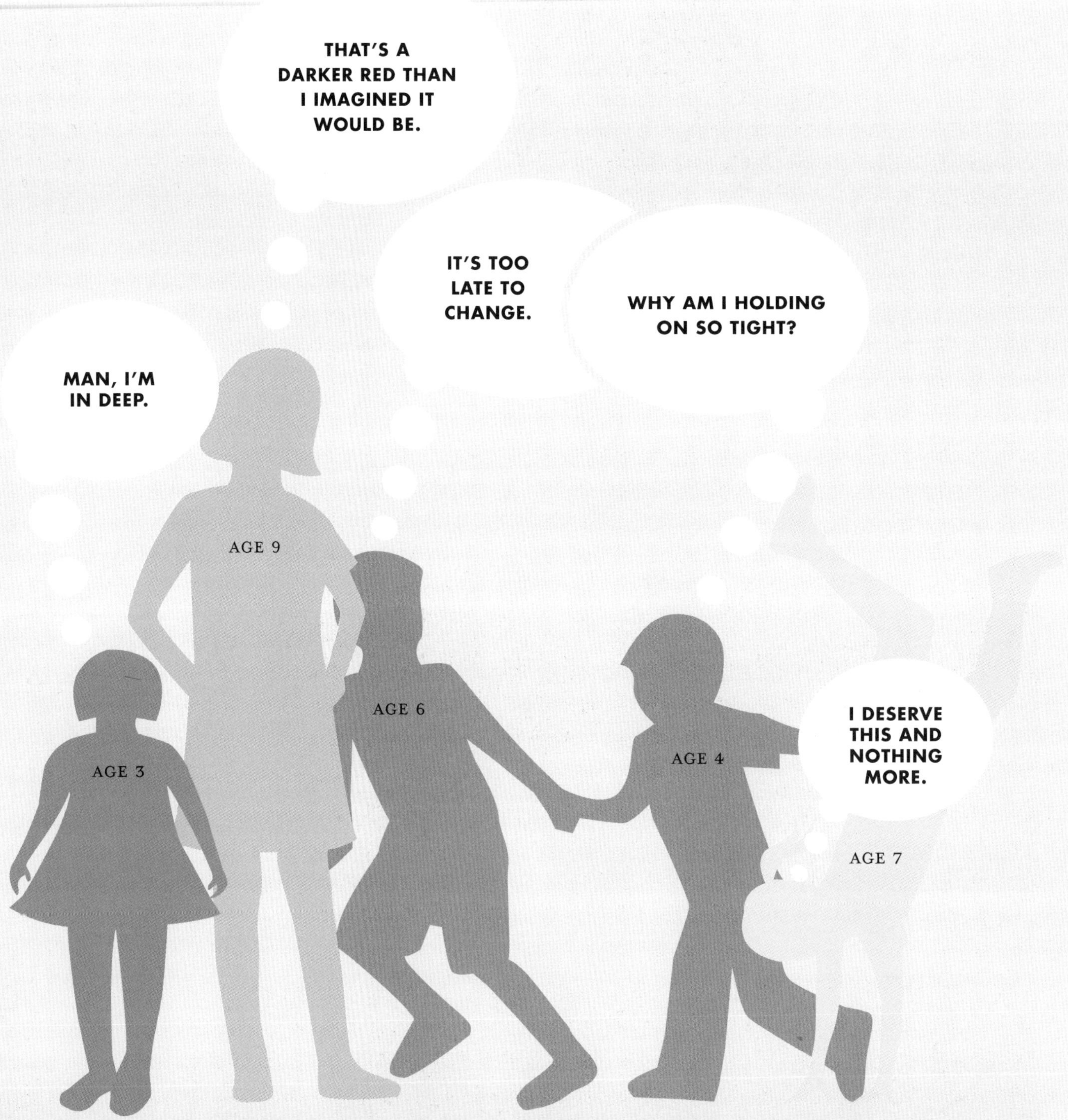

THAT'S A DARKER RED THAN I IMAGINED IT WOULD BE.

IT'S TOO LATE TO CHANGE.

WHY AM I HOLDING ON SO TIGHT?

MAN, I'M IN DEEP.

AGE 9

AGE 6

AGE 3

AGE 4

I DESERVE THIS AND NOTHING MORE.

AGE 7

LESS COMMON BUT STILL-COMMON THOUGHTS:

This result is getting to be less surprising.

What will hindsight say of this?

I hope this is the last time.

This is a worthy punishment.

Those doors are locked for a reason.

Used medical equipment has real value.

Who noticed that? Anyone? No one?

This will never work. I wish I didn't know this wouldn't work.

This will probably come back to bite me.

HOW THE ICE-CUBE INDUSTRY DAMAGES OUR GLACIERS AND LAW SCHOOLS

At precisely 4:35 a.m., every day, in the northeast province of Greenland aptly named Ittoqqortoormiit, workers in waterproof bibs and angry galoshes head outside to their chosen job. They work hard and are paid less than they're owed. But that's where your sympathy for these men should end. For the job of these workers is to do some of the greatest damage to our ecosystem of any human on earth: they are harvesting ice.

I like a cold Arnold Palmer on a hot afternoon the same as you. But did you know that each ice cube you consume is hastening the demise of this planet? The ice-cube industry is preying on our desperate and craven need for cold refreshment. Every time these environmental vultures mine into the cold ice shelfs of the Arctic Circle or ice floes of Newfoundland, they're digging a bit further into our planet's ever-shrinking future. I should have used a better metaphor there. You can't really dig into the future. I apologize for that. I am tired because I was up late last night, at a rave with some people I met at a rave.

The point is, in the process of this devastating mining, these greedy ice profiteers have completely decimated the habitats of hundreds of species, from the Spotted Glacier Snake to the Dimpled Icicle Grout. And do these corporate ice raiders care? They do not. The "icers," as they're known to the locals, sit in their trucks laughing all day long, helping themselves to ice cubes with gluttonous abandon — *sometimes even without drinks to put them in*. So next time you're at the Piggly Wiggly, about to buy a bag of ice — or, worse, *chopped ice: hear their screams!* — reflect on the fact that you're killing glaciers, other stuff, and animals. Some of those animals might have gone to law school. Think about that for a second. Animals admitted to *law school*, some pretty decent schools, dead because of you and your ice.

A newly built Slovenian ice-cube mining facility. As the saying goes, "Slovenia is a land where the ice cubes are nearly as perfect as the environmental degradation."

PLACES TO KEEP YOUR CHILDREN IN THE MORNING WHILE YOU ARE BUSY

When I speak at conferences of scientists inferior to me, they often ask me, "Dr. Doris, I have a question unrelated to your scientific work, and..." This is when I usually strike them with a club. When they regain consciousness, they often continue trying to ask me some inane question unrelated to my discoveries and theories. If I am unsuccessful in clubbing them again, or in enclosing them in soundproof boxes that can be shipped abroad, they occasionally manage to tell me that they have a child in their home, and that they don't know where to put this child while they are trying to have their breakfast. I think it's impossible in this short

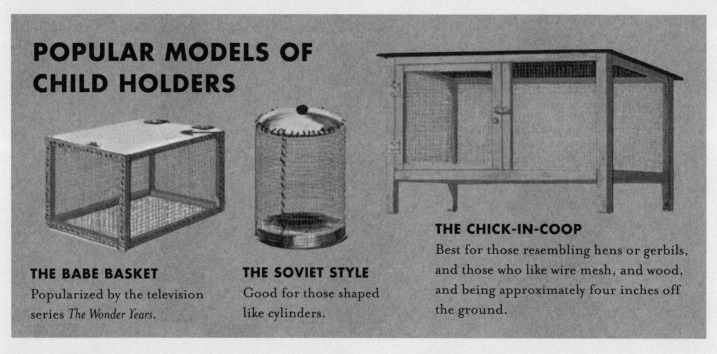

POPULAR MODELS OF CHILD HOLDERS

THE BABE BASKET
Popularized by the television series *The Wonder Years*.

THE SOVIET STYLE
Good for those shaped like cylinders.

THE CHICK-IN-COOP
Best for those resembling hens or gerbils, and those who like wire mesh, and wood, and being approximately four inches off the ground.

space to fully explore how idiotic this question is. First of all, why did they let the child into their home in the first place? If they can keep raccoons and other woodland creatures at bay, why not children? The child's mental capacity is similar to that of an outdoor rodent, after all, and thus children are as easy to control as ferrets and guinea pigs — two mammals, by the way, that make better pets than children. But if you do find yourself with a child at home, and you want to eat and read the paper in the morning undisturbed, then you need some kind of container. Many good containers are available at hardware stores, or can be easily constructed with chicken wire and wood. The key is that they MUST NOT HAVE A DOOR. A door will imply you will let them out if they whimper or scratch. If you do need to let the child out at some point, you can always use wire cutters. But why would you want to do that? And you don't *have* wire cutters, you say? Who are you, anyway? What sort of person has a child in their home, and then wants to limit its movements at certain times of day, and then doesn't have either a cage or a pair of wire cutters? My time is being wasted here.

SEVEN ANIMALS WHO WOULD RATHER NOT LIVE IN THE TUNDRA

Part of it was just misleading advertising. As it turns out, the word *spacious* can mean many things. Anyway, they bought in, now they want out. The following mammals will accept offers to house-sit or home-swap. They're also considering studying abroad. Or opening a bookshop in Greece. Maybe one of those little islands, where they could have a little store and sell books in English to tourists. Seems like that would work.

CARIBOU *Rangifer tarandus*

Is also regretting not finishing college.

ARCTIC FOX *Alopex lagopus*

It's not the cold, really. It's more the lack of basic services.

ARCTIC TERN *Sterna paradisaea*

Thought the tundra would be friendlier. But everyone's been so snobby.

POLAR BEAR *Ursus maritimus*

With a few cable channels, even Starz, this might be okay.

MUSK OX *Ovibos moschatus*

Part of it is feeling unappreciated. A little encouragement would go a long way.

ARCTIC HARE *Lepus arcticus*

It's really the loneliness. That's the problem, ultimately.

SNOWY OWL *Sterna paradisaea*

You know what would make a difference? A light jacket, something waterproof.

GRIZZLY BEAR *Ursus arctos*

You should never follow a girlfriend this far.

AREAS OF THE PLANET CONTROLLED BY CHILDREN

NATIONAL INSTITUTE OF POWERFUL SCIENCE AND WEAPONRY

No one knows what they're making here but it's probably bad.

MOST SAVANNAHS

Lions and other large mammals simply lease access from the child caretakers, who are unruly landlords.

HIDDEN MOUNTAIN LAIR CONTAINING ALL WORLD SECRETS

Children whisper them — secrets — constantly, and then catalog them here in this mountain. Imagine how hurtful billions of secrets, all kept in one hollowed-out mountain, are. They know they are hurtful but don't care.

PANAMA CANAL (AND ALL CANALS)

Children love canals. This is well-known. Few know that they control them using a worldwide network of pulleys and threats.

The Story of the Colossal Collapse of Canada's Tundraworld

The extremely rich are a troubled lot. By the time most have reached their financial zenith, their brains are usually minced and mashed to near unrecognizability. This lack of conventional brain workings makes them do strange, impulsive things. Some buy sports teams. Others, submarines. And some urinate on their money while drinking Sierra Mist.

And then there are the stupid ones.

Porty Jalock was a multimillionaire and Canadian — which, unfortunately, is a combination that remains possible. Porty loved many a thing. He loved birds of flight, games of chance, books of mystery, and twill. But most of all, he loved his native land. So much so that at the age of 45, he bought 1,200 acres of fine Canadian soil in Prince Edward Island with hopes of constructing an amusement park and monument to his favorite part of the Borealian countryside.

Believing that the cold, deep, dark, bitter, spiteful, and toothless cold he grew up in was the key to his success, Porty thought to reward his countrymen with the gift of a similar experience. Thus, spending all of his savings and that of his in-laws (they herded reindeer), he built Tundraworld.

"The land of frozen delight,"* said the tagline under the ads for Tundraworld. And truer words were never falsely advertised. There was no food, drink, or toilets allowed in Tundraworld ("to preserve authenticity," said Porty). Money, however, was allowed. Especially if it came in the form of Blizzard Bucks, printed in an austere shade of blue and picturing the severe, unsmiling face of a topcoated and monocled walrus.

The park, when it finally came to fruition, boasted 16 rides and diversions. These included: the Avalanche in a Small Room Challenge; the How Long Till You Freeze Snow Maze Adventure; and the aptly named Surviveland World, which consisted of a large fenced-in swath of inhospitable land, electric fences, hidden, spiky pitfalls, and two 300-ft., 100-grade Celsius hail machines.

Needless to say, though the weather at Tundraworld remained authentically bleak, ticket sales were even bleaker. But a good Canuckian is never outdone by such setbacks. Porty, in a last-ditch attempt to save his business, got through to the prime minister (through various political channels) and begged for a national holiday to celebrate Canada's chilly heritage. This, he argued, would save Canada's one and only great theme park. But the prime minister, an avid beach-volleyball enthusiast and loather of cold weather, rejected the plea. Porty was devastated.

He closed up shop that next morning and drove into the Canadian wild. No one knows how far he drove that day, or where he ended up. But the 1996 Canadian ban on all factual writing of any kind has made accurate reporting on the country's affairs impossible. However, the nonfiction ban has not been entirely without its merits. It has, for example, driven sales of the Canadian national T-shirt, CANADA, THE HOME OF ORAL HISTORY, through the roof. So, there's that.

Not to be confused with yogurt or ice cream delicacies.

HOW BEST TO PACK TUNDRA WHEN GOING ON A SHORT TRIP TO FORT MYERS

You have to go somewhere and you have to pack quickly. This is a normal enough situation. You've packed your radon and your tubing. You've packed your micro-collider and your prosthetics. You have your shirts and pants and serums that can inflict debilitating toothaches in the mouths of your enemies. But what about your tundra? First of all, you shouldn't have waited to pack your tundra last. The tundra is vast and cold and unforgiving — why wait to pack it? It doesn't matter now. Now we have to solve the problem. To start, remove everything else you've packed. Now disassemble your suitcase using pliers and a mallet. Now find a small dog and bring it into your home. Promise to feed and care for it. Tell the dog, "This is your forever home." Try to forget about the tundra, which, after all, broke your heart. A trip with the tundra won't bring you back together. Even in Cabo. It won't work. You have to acknowledge this and move on. You deserve better. You deserve a new life, a life where you can be yourself and not someone trying to please the tundra. You cannot please the tundra.

TUNDRA

WHAT KINDS OF FOOD PRODUCE
WHICH KINDS OF CHILDREN

FOOD	RESULT	COMMENTS
WHOLE MILK	BRUTISH THUGS	You chose the heavy, fully saturated dairy drink during your nine months of pregnancy, and now, 20 years later, you've got a thick-headed hooligan fencing diamond choke collars out of your living room. Was that extra fat really worth it?
DELI MEAT	CARNIES	Feed your fetus cold cuts and be assured that it will grow up to entice suckers into unwinnable games of chance. Beware these showy and foldable meats if you ever wish to see your offspring on Thanksgiving.
GOAT CHEESE	GRIFTERS	On the other hand, it's good to have at least one grifter in the family. Keeps you humble, and you'll have good stories to tell friends at parties. They talk about their cousin the professional cricketer, you talk about your daughter the grifter.
CANTALOUPE	CANNIBALS	You know how people talk about good cholesterol and bad cholesterol? Well, this is the my-son-consumes-human-flesh type of vitamin C. Stick to honeydew.
SUNFLOWER SEEDS	LIBERTARIANS	Is it worth it? The seeds are delicious, yes, but would you want to be responsible for the next Ron Paul? Think of the effect on the price of gold.

HOW TO FREEZE YOURSELF FOR THE FUTURE

You might as well. It's safer than waiting.

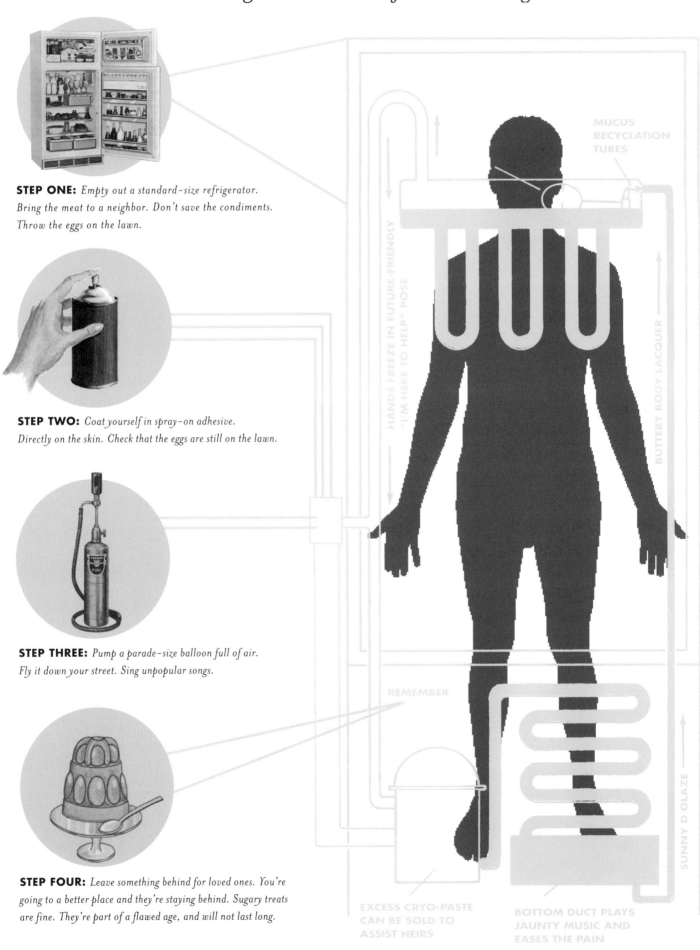

STEP ONE: *Empty out a standard-size refrigerator. Bring the meat to a neighbor. Don't save the condiments. Throw the eggs on the lawn.*

STEP TWO: *Coat yourself in spray-on adhesive. Directly on the skin. Check that the eggs are still on the lawn.*

STEP THREE: *Pump a parade-size balloon full of air. Fly it down your street. Sing unpopular songs.*

STEP FOUR: *Leave something behind for loved ones. You're going to a better place and they're staying behind. Sugary treats are fine. They're part of a flawed age, and will not last long.*

MUCUS RECYCLATION TUBES

HANDS FREEZE IN FUTURE-FRIENDLY "I'M HERE TO HELP" POSE

BUTTERY BODY LACQUER

REMEMBER

SUNNY D GLAZE

EXCESS CRYO-PASTE CAN BE SOLD TO ASSIST HEIRS

BOTTOM DUCT PLAYS JAUNTY MUSIC AND EASES THE PAIN

RELATED QUESTION: WHY ARE FROZEN PEOPLE PRETTIER THAN REGULAR PEOPLE?

Many humans and similar creatures have been found frozen in the tundra, and most researchers believe that the tundra's tendency to be very cold often contributes to people getting frozen there. So we know that much. Good. But one question remains: why are so many frozen people so excellent looking? Gorgeous, even. They look so good, and so stylish and confident. It really is something to see, these wonderful-looking people frozen in blocks of ice, and dead for thousands or even tens of thousands of years. What and why?

FIVE THEORIES

BORING THEORY: The beautiful are bold and thus they are the most likely to travel to frozen regions to discover, conquer, and breed. But then they get frozen.

OTHER THEORY: Ice, over time, freezes our outermost, loudest, flawed features, in a process similar to the treatment of warts. Once frozen, these features, like bulbous noses and ears and foreheads, begin to chip and fall off. This leaves the frozen with only their stronger, inner layers of prettiness remaining.

BIG LAST THEORY: Anticipating a time in the distant future when our civilization is eradicated from Earth, various world governments united in a conspiracy to plant these splendid-looking human specimens in an effort to show future cultures studying our extinct civilization that, say what you will, if nothing else, at least we had some good looking dudes.

If You're Assembling a Four-Member Team to Survey a Tract of Land for a Possible Mixed-Use Development, You Need... an Australian™

It's Better with an Australian™

Studies show that work sites are safer, cleaner, and more efficient when two or more Australians are involved. Even if it's just the catering.

Do not take Australians if you take nitrates, often prescribed for chest pain, as this may cause a sudden, unsafe drop in blood pressure. Discuss your general health status with your doctor to ensure that you are healthy enough to engage with an Australian. If you experience chest pain, nausea, or any other discomforts during your time with an Australian, seek immediate medical help. In the rare instance of an Australian lasting more than four hours, seek immediate medical help to avoid long-term injury. If you are older than 65, or have serious liver or kidney problems, your doctor may start you at the lowest dose of Australians. If you are taking protease inhibitors, your doctor may limit you to a maximum single dose of Australian in a 24-hour period. In rare instances, Australians will cause a sudden decrease in or loss of vision. It is not possible to determine whether these events are related directly to Australians or to other factors. Australians should not be used in conjunction with other Pacific Rim peoples. The most common side effects of Australians are headache, facial flushing, bluish vision, and sensitivity to light. You are encouraged to report negative side effects of Australians to the Australian Department of Labor, and to Andrew Adamson.

CRAIG DOOLITTLE, WHO COULD TALK TO A COUPLE ANIMALS

Many things are tough in life. Methanol distillation, for instance. Another is following in the footsteps of a legend. Especially when the legend is your father, the beloved Doctor John Doolittle, and when you're allergic to dander. Such was the fate of a small, fur-fearing boy called Craig.

One Sunday, Craig Doolittle, ripened to the age of eight, looked at his father effortlessly debating a Shetland sheepdog about tomatillo harvesting. In that moment, with the sun on his face and sweaty raisins in his pockets, Craig become aware that never in his life would he be able to touch or understand this blessed animal, or any animals, the way his father could. There were, in fact, only two creatures Craig could talk to: stag beetles and regular beetles.

Craig could have bemoaned this short straw the world had offered him, but Craig was no such empty-glassed pessimist. While lacking in most of the genetic makeup that made his father so gifted and sought-after, Craig still observed that an ever-so-slight amount of talent had dribbled down into his DNA. And he wasn't about to let this go to waste. Even though no one cared, at all, about stag beetles or regular beetles, or what they had to say.

I, Dr. Doris, met this young man at a conference where I was presenting a paper that everyone argued about but secretly thought was awesome. He was standing outside the convention hall, trying to get funding for some research — a study about the emotional lives of stag beetles and regular beetles. I felt for the kid. I remember him wearing a page-boy hat. There might have been a dog reading over his shoulder, I don't know. But I do know I felt like he'd never amount to anything, dressed like that, with his weirdly wrinkled hands, and reading some book that had the title on the back cover. Why was he reading a book about Dog Language while asking for money to study beetles? It was really a matter of messaging.

Craig Doolittle is now the head of Chevron.

WHAT CAN BE DONE ABOUT CHILDREN AND THEIR ATTRIBUTES?

Including:

THEIR ANNOYING
LAUGHS

THEIR CHIRPY WAY OF
TALKING

THEIR FREQUENT
OUTBURSTS OF
INEXPLICABLE EMOTION

THEIR LOATHESOME
CLOTHES

THEIR UNBOUNDED
NEEDINESS

THEIR TINY FEET
AND SHOES

THEIR HORRIFYING
LITTLE TEETH

THEIR NEED TO
BREAK THINGS

THEIR NEED TO PAINT
TIRESOME LITTLE
PAINTINGS OF
NOTHING AT ALL

THEIR LOVE OF HORSES
AND RAINBOWS
AND RELATIVES

THEIR EXCITEMENT
ABOUT THINGS

THEIR FAT LITTLE HANDS

THEIR NEED FOR
SHELTER AND CONSTANT
CARE FOR UPWARDS
OF 18 YEARS

These are some of the questions that have plagued humankind for the many hundreds of years that we have been burdened with the phenomenon of children. None of these traits seem necessary or serve any evolutionary purpose. Indeed, there are so many aspects of children I find unreasonable that studying them at all is very tiring, and frequently onerous. The one thing I do like about children is their gullibility. I, and many other adults and scientists and teachers, have been able to tell them virtually anything, and they have believed it. They believe the thing about the planets and how we're the only one with life on it. They believe the thing about how much smarter they are than other mammals and crustaceans. And they believe all they hear about hope, love, goodness, and tomorrow. This willingness to believe makes much of our work as adults — our filthy, filthy work, our wretched but essential work, however filthy — far easier.

THE GIRL TOO BORING TO WRITE ABOUT

Nancy was eight years old. Then, later, she was nine, ten, and eleven. The point is that Nancy was dull. Painfully and preternaturally dull. A dullard through and through. And yet even if one were to craft a tale about how dull people can be, one still wouldn't pick Nancy to write about. That's because Marcia Druthers already had that honor (see *The Current Happenings of Not Much at All*, London: Breethchaps & Brothers, 1931, pp. 11–442).

The problem with boring Nancy Koploski was that even her boring features were too boring to comment on. Some bland people, like Davy McNulty, had exciting, interesting facets to their boringness. For Davy, being boring was almost an art. People marveled at his lack of interesting qualities. Nancy, on the other hand, let her boringness grow and fester — like a bubbling neck boil.

Nancy moved around *just enough* to avoid being a good study in laziness. She talked *just enough* to prevent concern that she had a fear of talking. And she had *just enough* competent thought-like musings to remove herself from any need of special assistance. She just sat there, making quiet, thoughtful, boring faces.

Nancy was perfectly undocumentable. Like one of those plants no one can decide if it's a weed or a flower, but then they figure, "Why bother finding out?" Nancy Koploski was just short of deserving further investigation. At this point you probably wish you were bored by Nancy's boringness, so you could call up a friend and tell him or her, "Let me tell you about this horrifically boring girl," but she blew even that opportunity.

Do not be fooled by this colorful illustration at right. Nancy is more boring than it suggests.

* Upon completing her reading of this case study to approve it for publication, Nancy simply shrugged, adjusted the pillow under her back slightly to the left, almost crossed her legs, and blinked.

THOSE WHO WERE NEVER CHILDREN

O f all the horrible afflictions the world can give us — both those afflictions thrust upon us and those we rightly earned — perhaps none is worse than having been young. As we age, and improve greatly with age, we still carry the burden of knowing that we were once of no value to anyone. We were children.

But some were lucky. They never experienced this period. They simply arrived, just as some deities and meals arrive — hot and ready to enjoy with cider.

Among the things they were spared: crying, collages, the President's Physical Fitness Test, and play-ground slides made of steel that retain the sun's great heat and scorch hands and legs.

All of these people were drawn against green backgrounds.

JOSEPH B. HAROLD   R.L. MONTGOMERY   THIS MAN   ALSO THIS MAN

MAXWELL R. BOYLE   THIS MAN!   GIOVANNI I. MARCUS   THIS WOMAN!

NEVER A CHILD!   NOT A CHILD!   BOTH NOT CHILDREN!

TUNDRA ON A MELANCHOLY DAY

Everyone has such days, but the tundra has them more than most. Sometimes, despite the gloomy weather, the constant cold and wind, and the lack of much of anything to look at, the tundra can feel a bit dispirited. What is the point, the tundra thinks, of days like this? And so the tundra will eat margarine from the tub. The tundra will shuffle to and fro without fully tying its shoes. The tundra will not shower. The tundra will not answer the phone. The tundra will pick up a book, thinking for a moment that a day like this is made for quiet reading and contemplation, only to become, moments later, bored and distracted. The tundra will finally try to call its brother Steve, who lives in Phoenix. Steve will not pick up his phone, and this will get the tundra more dispirited. The tundra will know that if it goes to the gym to exercise, the endorphins might solve its problem, but it will not be able to get itself together enough to get to the gym. The tundra will look up at the sky, a watercolor mess of gray and white and gray. The tundra will sigh audibly, and then laugh at its own theatricality. The tundra will scratch itself and again laugh, this time at its lack of decorum. The tundra will think of a movie it once saw, called *Tron*, and then will go buy *Tron*, for under ten dollars, at Best Buy. Then the tundra will watch *Tron*, and when *Tron* is over, the tundra will be energized, inspired, determined that it, too, can save a secret world from oppression or dissolution. If only it could get to an arcade. Where is there an arcade? the tundra wonders. And where is Bruce Boxleitner? And this question will get the tundra sad again.

COMMON QUESTIONS OF CHILDREN

Why aren't I being taxed?

When can I start owning property?

Whose cuff links are these? Mine?

Do I come across as sympathetic?

What kind of lacquer does rosewood call for?

You're positive you haven't seen my cuff links?

What's the escape clause?

What's the buyout?

Why are you sitting at my desk?

Are these fish happier
than I am?

IN CLOSING

Now you know the truth about the world's coldest regions: the heart of children. You have also learned how and what lives in the tundra and why no one ever bothers to speak of it. Now you can find a sturdy box, empty all this information inside it, and give it to Steve.

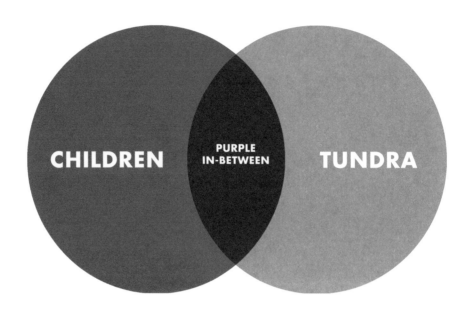

UPCOMING TITLES FROM THE H-O-W SERIES*

TUNNELING FOR PROFIT

OUTDOOR TABLES AND CHAIRS: BEYOND THE HYPE

WORKING WITH DAIRY PRODUCTS TO ACHIEVE NATION-BUILDING

HOBOKEN: WHY?

SUPERFLUOUS ANIMALS AND PLANTS AND HOW TO THIN THE HERD

CLASPS AND THEIR DETRACTORS

HISTORY OF STRIPES AND STRIPED THINGS

PAPUA NEW GUINEA: SURE, OKAY

1,000 OTHER USES FOR SCISSORS

ROYALTY AROUND THE WORLD AND HOW TO TELL JOKES ABOUT THEM

HOW TO BUILD A MOUNTAIN

CLINT EASTWOOD AND HIS WIVES

THE ART OF FOLDING JACKETS

ARE WE IN THE GOLDEN YEARS OF PINCHING?

TRIPE SANDWICHES AND OTHER WAYS OF KNOWING YOU MIGHT NOT BE WANTED

FAST BULLETS AND THE GUNS WHO LOVE THEM

CELEBRITIES AND THEIR FAVORITE DOGMAS

THE SORDID, DEBASED LIVES OF CARP-PACKAGING ASSEMBLYLINERS

THE WHO, WHAT, WHEN, AND WHERE OF AMERICAN SAMOA

CANOPIES?

NO MORE CANOPIES

REGULATORS PICK THEIR FAVORITE REGULATIONS

NO ONE WILL NOTICE: WHEN YOU USE BAMBOO

CALICO THINGS

KOFI ANNAN'S AUTO REPAIR HEAVEN

YOUR WRETCHED REFLECTION: 100 CANADIANS COMMENT ON YOUR STUPID FACE

SALAD FOR BREAKFAST, TEA FOR DESSERT: 40 FAST AND EASY RECIPES FOR ELDERLY RETIRED LAB TECHNICIANS

subject to change and becoming better

ABOUT THE AUTHORS

Dr. Doris Haggis-On-Whey has 32 degrees from 31 universities and colleges, most of them in countries better than yours. She has discovered most things on her own, and rediscovered many other things that were improperly discovered the first time around. She has been honored with many honors, including the Honorable Honor of All Honors Honor, which is a pretty good one to get, and is awarded only when absolutely necessary. The author of more than 179 books on twice as many subjects, Dr. Doris is currently working on a book that will summarize all of her previous books, while also rendering every other scientific text ever published superfluous and even funny. She is widely credited with originating the following ideas and theories: the idea that water should be wet; the idea that rain should fall down, as opposed to some other idiotic way; the idea that food should be edible and not some other idiotic thing; and the idea that Kansas City should be in Missouri, not Kansas. She lives in Crumpets-Under-Kilt, Scotland, with no pets and Benny.

ABOUT THE DESIGNER

Lauren LoPrete has no natural camouflage or defense capabilities. She also cannot read a thermostat. But she is a skilled obeyer and good at packing. She should be spared.

Research assistance has been provided by the de la Manzana brothers, and by Toph Eggers and also Dave Eggers.